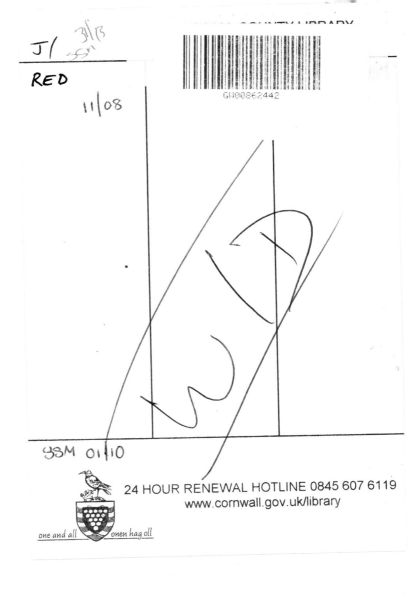

*Portrait of Antony Payne, courtesy of the
Royal Cornwall Museum, Truro*

*Copy can also be seen in the courtyard of
The Tree Inn, Stratton, Cornwall*

Antony Payne
Last of the Cornish Giants

by
J. E. Pain

authorHOUSE®

AuthorHouse™ UK Ltd.
500 Avebury Boulevard
Central Milton Keynes, MK9 2BE
www.authorhouse.co.uk
Phone: 08001974150

First published by AuthorHouse 10/9/2008

ISBN: 978-1-4389-0184-8 (sc)

Printed in the United States of America
Bloomington, Indiana

This book is printed on acid-free paper.

For Kary

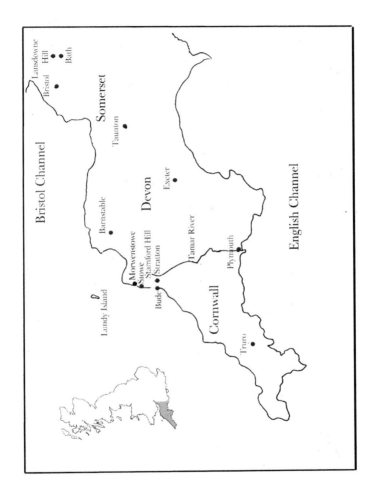

Lansdowne Hill • Bath
Bristol •

Somerset

Bristol Channel

Taunton •

Devon

Exeter •

Barnstable •

Morwenstowe
Stowe
Stamford Hill
Stratton •

Tamar River

Plymouth •

English Channel

Lundy Island

Bude •

Cornwall

Truro •

CONTENTS

PREFACE

During a stay in Stratton, Cornwall, I happened to visit The Tree Inn. There in the courtyard was an enormous framed copy of an oil portrait of Antony Payne, the man they call 'The Last of the Cornish Giants'. My eight year old daughter was fascinated. Unfortunately we found that there was no book for children on a most suitable subject - a boy and a giant winning the day.

Little is written about the real Antony Payne besides registry dates and the facts of his one great act of heroism during the Civil War when his master, Sir Beville Grenville was killed in battle and his troops were about to run away. Antony pulled Sir Beville's fifteen year old son John up onto his father's horse and led the troops to victory for the King, shouting 'A Grenville leads you still!'. For this he was honoured when King Charles II returned to the throne: the King himself commissioned the life-sized portrait of the giant.

There are facts and legends that make up his story. The Church register in Stratton records his birth in 1610. Legend says that he quickly grew into a larger than average lad whose back was so broad that the other children could use it for a chalk board, that his cradle was used as a fishing boat and many other exaggerations. At any rate, he was bound to the Grenville's household at Stowe, four miles from Stratton, in 1619 when he was just a boy.

Letters between Sir Beville and his wife Grace tell many things about life at Stowe. Sir Beville was often away in London but he cared deeply about his crops and horses and of course his family. Sir Beville supplied a teacher for the local children because of his strong belief in universal education. Antony would have taken his lessons at Stowe with the others. When later he invited the sons of his neighbours to share the tutors he hired for his own children, they called it Sir Beville's academy. As a young man, the giant was to teach these boys riding, shooting, fencing, and fishing, which Sir Beville referred to as 'gentlemanly sports'.

Because Antony's life was part of the Grenville's I have inserted him there, accompanying Richard to Oxford and back, helping the family to move house, and helping to raise an army for the king. When war broke out Antony became Sir Beville's personal body guard and tutor for young Jack who joined the army when he was just 13.

Being in the army didn't mean being far from home. Sir Beville and his brother Richard were defending Cornwall and part of Devon for the King. Before the Battle of Stamford Hill, for example, the troops waited for days in Stratton. They might have spent their evenings in the public houses there, playing games - some we still play today, some almost forgotten.

Sir Beville Grenville died at the Battle of Lansdown. A letter which is said to have been written by Antony to Lady Grace in sympathy was really most likely written centuries later by the Rev. S. Hawker of Morwenstow. Hawker was a writer and although he claimed to have found the letter in a trunk with other Grenville letters, the style is very like Hawker's. Genuine or not, this letter has become part of the story of Antony Payne.

No one knows what happened to the giant when Jack, now Sir John, fled to France and later to Jersey. Antony may have gone with him. When Charles II came back to the throne, however, Antony was made a Yeoman of the Guard and Harbinger of the Arms, and stationed with Sir John at Plymouth where his portrait was painted. He must have returned to Stowe when the new house was built because on a visit there the King's secretary noted in his diary that 'the King was amused' to see Antony Payne dusting the tester of the Golden Bed. This had been made for Catherine of Aragon, the first wife of Henry VIII. Queen Elizabeth I had made a gift of it to an earlier Sir Richard Grenville.

Stratton's church records show that Antony Payne and his wife, Sebella, died within four days of each other in 1691 and were buried there. The manor house where they lived is now The Tree Inn. His body was so large that they had to cut a hole in the floor to lower it because they couldn't carry it down the stairs.

It was said that he was buried beneath an aisle in the church - an honour indeed. This may have been proven when a lead coffin containing a man over seven feet tall was found during renovations of the Church's foundations in Victorian times. Unfortunately it was reburied in the churchyard without a marker.

This is the story of Antony Payne - a mix of fact and legend with just a dash of popular belief. This is probably exactly the way a giant should be remembered.

CHAPTER 1
A LUCKY SPIDER

Antony Payne opened his eyes to the hazy morning sun coming through the tiny window of the loft. He lay on his back and watched as a spider busily worked her web across it. As the light caught on the fine threads they shone like silver. A lucky spider, he thought. This would be a lucky day.

He looked about him. The little room under the thatched roof was just big enough for three straw mattresses. Two of these were empty. He scrambled out of bed and began pulling on his patched breeches. They no longer met around his middle so he tied them with a cord. His brothers must already be down eating breakfast and if he didn't hurry there would be nothing left for him to eat. He struggled into his dirty shirt that had once belonged to his father then hurried down the ladder to the main room where the family were gathered.

'Your mother called you twice, Tony,' his father said sternly without looking up. 'See that you get up with the rest of us. Now eat.'

Tony hurried to his place and began to fill his bowl from the nearly empty pot in the centre of the table. The barley porridge was thin but warm and felt good in his empty stomach. He ate in silence.

By the fire his mother was feeding baby Rose while three year old Catherine whined and pulled at her skirts. Rose began to cry. His father scowled and his brothers left the table. His mother looked over at Tony and her lips pressed into a thin straight line.

Something peculiar had been happening to Tony that his family couldn't ignore. He was growing very big and at nine years old was already as tall as his father. Keeping him clothed and fed had become a major worry for the Paynes who were poor tenant farmers. And despite his size the boy was weak and complained of his arms and legs aching so he was no use on the farm. The jeers and mockery of his older brothers Simon and Andrew made him shy and clumsy as well. It was easy to forget his age and his mother had no patience with him.

'Tony, you'll pick bramble berries along the hedges today,' his mother ordered, placing her big market basket squarely on the end of the table. She put a large slice of bread and a little cheese in it for his lunch. 'If that maude isn't full I'll want to know why. You're big enough to reach the ones the others can't get at. And don't you go eating them all either,' she added severely.

Tony quickly picked up the basket and left without looking up at his mother. He kept walking until he came to the road to Poughill Mill. Here the ripe blackberries were everywhere along both sides of the road and he was soon lost in his thoughts. Where did the roads go? This way would go to the sea eventually, but the road continued along the coast. Where would he end up if he just kept walking? He had heard of the market in Bideford and of course he had heard of the great city of London but these were only names to a boy whose life had been spent on a farm by the river a mile from sleepy Stratton.

He left his basket on the deserted road. Thinking had made him hungry and the berries now went unconsciously into his mouth. He walked along the winding road, thinking and picking and eating until

3

a clatter of horses' hooves brought him to his senses and he looked around wildly for the basket.

It was too late. The riders had come around the bend and seen it too late. In their attempt to stop, one of the horses had reared up, coming down smack in the middle of all his berries. Tony gave a cry as the basket crunched under the stumbling horse and berries scattered all over the road.

'Is this your basket?' The rider asked crossly as he dismounted. He was a well dressed gentleman of about fifty with a terrifying air of authority. Because of Tony's size the man took him for someone old enough to know better than to be so careless on a public road. 'You nearly caused an accident! What do you have to say for yourself?'

'Well sir...' Tony stammered in a boyish squeak, too frightened to think.

The second rider dismounted, a man in his mid-twenties and both men looked carefully at the person cowering in front of them who was equally as tall as they were.

'My mother will save you the trouble of beating me, sirs, for when she hears about her market basket and my days work gone she'll be in a right old temper,' Tony blurted out helplessly and began to cry. The men exchanged puzzled looks.

'What is your name, young man,' the older gentleman asked, 'and how old are you?'

'My name is Antony Payne and I have had my ninth birthday,' the boy replied obediently, hoping for the best.

'Well Antony Payne, here's something for your mother's market basket,' he said placing a silver coin in the astonished boy's hand, 'and here's something for the berries,' he added a copper coin beside the silver one and smiled. 'You'll be a marvellous great man someday.' With that the men mounted up and rode on.

Tony stood holding the money tight in his fist, as if it might somehow escape of it's own accord and follow the horsemen. After a long moment he looked down at the basket. It was bent and the handle broken but the bottom was still sound. His bread and cheese were only slightly bent. He put his lunch and the coins in the basket and began to save as many of the berries as he could. Then began picking with a fury.

Later as he lay on the hillside looking down over Stratton he thought about what he would say when he got home. The men were kind and his mother would be happy to have the money. A silver coin would buy much more than a basket and he would be bringing berries after all.

His mother's face lit up with real happiness when she saw the money. The story of the horsemen and the coins had to be told over and over.

His brother's weren't at all impressed.

'Well,' sighed Andrew sarcastically, 'at least we have a use for him now. We can send him out and travellers will pay money to look at him. You're a freak, Tony, so you'd better get used to it.'

'That's enough,' said his father sternly. But he thought, how big will he ever grow?

Tony saw his parents eyes turn away. A lump came to his throat. His brother's words cut into his mind and they would haunt him all his life.

'I'll go wooding,' he said gruffly, and hurried out to pick up sticks where no one could see him cry. There was no one who was kind, no one who smiled at him and no one he could talk to about his feelings but because he never had any of these, he didn't know why he felt so bad, only that he did. He took his armload of sticks and went back to the house.

'Tony, I want you to wash up and put on the clean shirt. You and your father are going to Stratton,' his mother greeted him, taking the wood from his arms in her usual tired manner. The baby began to fuss and she hurried to quiet her.

The boy was excited. It must have been because of the money he was getting such a treat. It seemed a little late in the day and it wasn't market day but his father probably had some business.

'I want you to be good,' his mother said sternly as he followed his father.

It was late afternoon when they stood at the large wooden gates of the Grenville's manor in Stratton. The father knocked on the small door in the gate and at last an old man opened it and peered at them.

'Aye, what can I do for you?' he asked.

'I was wanting to speak with the master, if I might. I believe he's here on business at Stratton today. He met my boy this morning.'

The old man looked curiously at Tony and stood aside. Tony found himself standing under a covered arch with a courtyard and stables in front of him. To his left was a door through which the old man had vanished, but to his right was an open door and window from which came the most wonderful smell of roast meat. And Tony was very hungry.

'He'll see you now,' the old man beckoned from the door.

'Wait here,' his father ordered Tony.

'Would you like to come in to wait?' a rosy faced cook came to the kitchen door to ask. She had been watching the visitors. 'I'll bet you'd like a bite to eat.'

Tony didn't have to be asked twice. The kitchen was a large room with two fireplaces and a big clomb oven for baking bread. He now saw the big roast of pork he'd smelled outside and pies and pastries on the table besides. The busy little woman motioned him to take a seat by the table and put two fruit tarts before him.

'Thank you, ma'am,' said Tony, stuffing the tarts quickly into his mouth before his father could return and take him away from this heaven.

The cook watched him curiously as he didn't seem to be either boy or man and kindly put a third tart before him. She did like a fellow who appreciated her cooking, she smiled to herself.

'What's your name?' she asked as she chopped vegetables and dropped them by handfuls into a pot.

'Tony, ma'am.'

'Your ma certainly has fed you well now, hasn't she?' The cook smiled encouragingly but Tony wasn't used to speaking much and just kept looking at the marvels of the well-stocked kitchen. "I suppose your pa's got farming business with the master," she went on. "Most folks do if they come here."

After a long and silent wait the old man came to the door and motioned for Tony to follow him. Through the other door was a room which seemed to be the grandest he had ever imagined. Draperies hung at the windows and carpets were under his bare feet. His father was standing near a table where sat the very man who had given Tony the coins. Beside him stood the younger man. Sir Bernard and his son Sir Beville Grenville smiled kindly.

'Antony,' Sir Bernard began, 'your father and I have been discussing your future. I told him that I think you will be a very fine man someday and I'd like to have you work for me.' He paused and looked thoughtfully at his son. Then he asked, 'Would you like to come to live and work at Stowe, Tony?"

No one had ever asked him how he felt about anything and now he was confused and frightened about what this meant, what would happen next.

Sir Bernard spoke again. 'You will have a warm bed, good food and clothing and you will learn a trade. You will do such jobs here as you can. When you are older you will have some wages. For the present my son would like you to learn to read, which will be your reward.'

Tony thought of the kitchen, the smiling rosy cook, the silver coin and said simply, 'I would like that, sir.'

'Say goodbye to your father then. You'll see him again soon, I'm sure. Cook will get you some supper and Old Harold will show you around.' And with that it was done.

As the door through the heavy gates closed and Tony turned to the kitchen door his thoughts went back to the lucky spider. It had been a lucky day after all.

CHAPTER 2
TAMING A GIANT

Stowe was an ancient house, built high on the cliffs overlooking the Cornish coast. It was described once as 'half dwelling, half castle' but it wasn't a forbidding place really. To the west was the sea, to the east was the rolling Coombe Valley. On three sides the old castle walls still stood with turrets and openings for dropping rocks or fiery oil on invaders. But on the fourth side the wall had been taken down to make a flower garden, decorated with statues and protected by clipped yew and holly hedges. There had once been a Norman keep in Medieval times, but that part had been replaced with a Tudor beamed front and windows with leaded diamond shaped panes.

Behind the house and down the hill were the barns and stables where Tony shared a room with the older gardeners, Brute and Joe. He was now fifteen, learning to graft pears and apples and to tend the orchards. He was happy at this work. It was a job he seemed to be made for. Tony was nearly seven feet tall now and this was a big advantage to be able to trim the trees and hedges without a ladder.

There was a not so pleasant side to his life, however, and that was the schoolroom. Sir Beville had arranged for a school master to teach the local children. He was a man who believed in education for everyone and had especially encouraged Tony to go to classes. He thought the boy must be lonely and hoped he might make some friends. But Sir Beville was often away in London and didn't know how this was to turn out.

It began one afternoon in the orchard when most of the tenants were picking the apple harvest. Two of Tony classmates were picking up the fruit that Tony had shaken from the tree.

'I've heard tell you can hold a bushel of corn in one of his stockings,' said one with a wink.

Tony began to blush the colour of the apples he was picking.

'You know they still use his cradle - for a fishing boat!' The other guffawed.

Tony gave the tree a great shake and apples rained everywhere. The boys ran away laughing. But the teasing continued and soon there were all sorts of fantastic stories to torment the shy giant. He wanted to please Sir Beville by learning but it was hard to be picked on day after day.

'I swear it was as big as Tony Payne's foot.'

'No, never that big!'

Tony liked to arrive early when no one was about. He would pick up a hornbook - a wooden paddle with square paper pages attached which you read by holding it up by the handle - and do his reading lesson in peace. He hardly noticed when the other children began to come in. Lessons lasted only an hour or two but they seemed to go on forever.

After school one day a group of his classmates waited for him. One of the boys called out, 'Nice of you to help with our lessons, Tony!' The group parted to let him pass but a gale of laughter broke out as they circled him. He turned round and round, red-faced and confused.

'Didn't want to forget our lessons, see,' someone called as he stumbled through the ring of children, 'so we used your back as a chalkboard. No sense in that much blank space going to waste.'

Everyone was laughing. Tony stood still. He had been proud of his leather waistcoat, given to him by Joe, the gardener. What had they put on it? A new sensation crept over him blotting out all the feelings of unhappiness. It was anger.

The next day Tony didn't go to the schoolroom in the big house. He turned instead and walked away along the cliff path, then down the loose grey shale to the beach. The tide was pulling out, leaving little pools of crystal clear water between the long, jagged fingers of rock that reached out to claw at the waves. Looking at the horizon he could see Lundy Island dark but clear. It was a sign of bad weather, he knew.

He carefully stepped over the smooth blue grey rocks until he came to one of the little rock pools and squatted beside it. The water in the pool was deep and still and he could see clearly the pale pink and green anemones looking like coloured fluff against the dark green kelp. Sandy pyramid shaped limpets and dark blue mussels clung to the stone basin while tiny

16

fish darted in and out of the kelp cover. Slowly he put his hand into the cold water and after a minute they began to swim between his fingers.

With a quick grab he pulled up a limpet. You had to be fast or they would pull themselves tight against the rock. He examined the unlucky limpet carefully.

Turning it upside down he gently pressed the soft, leathery bottom and two horn shaped feelers popped out and began to explore his thumb. Tony felt ashamed of himself and put the limpet back into the water. He watched until it had settled back on the side of the rock before walking on, stepping carefully from rock to slippery rock.

Around a bend he came on a mound of fallen boulders. Their size made him feel small and he could hide easily between them. He imagined he was a smuggler, waiting for a ship to pull in and fell asleep. When he woke the sun was hazy gold on the water and he could no longer see Lundy. The tide was coming in and he started for home.

As he made his way up the steep path to the cliff top he stopped. Ahead stood a group of his classmates. His long hair hung wet and sticky from the salty sea spray and his short trousers and patched shirt were covered with sand. Now he felt as if he had been left by the waves in a strange land with unfriendly natives. The boys began to laugh.

'How are you going to grow a brain if you don't come to school?' called one.

'We don't have a chalkboard without your back,' taunted another.

A strange feeling came over Tony as he stood there. They were wrong to keep making fun of him. And they shouldn't make him afraid to go to school. He lowered his head and walked slowly toward them. He would walk through them. He was much bigger than they were. Suddenly a large stone hit him in the head and blood came trickling down his face.

This was too much even for the giant's gentle nature. With a shout that was almost like a roar he ran towards them, not knowing what he was going to do. They didn't run, they just stood frozen with surprise. In an instant he had picked one up under each arm, carrying them up and along the cliff as if they were two little pigs. The others ran away screaming for help. He stopped and held them over the edge so they could see the jagged rocks below.

'Tony! Please don't kill us, Tony!'

Suddenly a sharp voice commanded, 'Put those boys down, now!' Lady Grace Grenville was storming up the cliff path toward Tony. She was small and blond and dressed in pale pink, but her blue eyes looked black with anger and there was no doubt that she intended to be obeyed. She walked right up to the startled giant and stood with her head back, looking up into his tear-streaked face.

Carefully he put the boys down. Lady Grace turned to them and said sharply, 'This is an end to your teasing. Is that clear? Now go home all of you!'

She stood only as high as Tony's chest but with the wind whipping her skirts and her voice strong and angry she seemed very powerful indeed. If the sea were a lady, Tony thought, she would be just like Lady Grace. No wonder sailors feared and loved the ocean.

'Come with me,' she ordered Tony. He was suddenly afraid. Although he had never been mistreated at Stowe he felt sure that they would beat him now. Perhaps he would be sent back to Stratton and his family would be ashamed of him.

They entered the house and Lady Grace led him to a small sitting room where a fire burned at one end and two comfortable chairs sat before a window that looked out onto the front garden and beyond. Lady Grace motioned for him to sit down.

'Now,' she began, picking up her embroidery, 'would you like to explain just what was going on out there?' She kept her eyes on her work as Tony explained as best he could all that had happened. He couldn't think how to put his feelings into words: the feeling of being different and not anybody's friend, the feeling of not knowing what to do to make things any better.

He felt ashamed for what he had done, but he wanted Lady Grace to understand his side of it.

'I'm truly sorry, my Lady,' he hung his head. 'I only meant to frighten them. I couldn't have lived with myself if one of them had gone over.'

Lady Grace was quiet for a long while. She knew her husband valued Tony as a kind and intelligent boy. What would he do about this? Well, he wasn't here and she would have to use her own judgement. She could see that he shouldn't continue in these classes - things could only get worse. She must think whether he had had enough education.

'Do you enjoy your lessons, Tony?' She asked curiously. His face brightened.

'Aye, that I do, my lady,' he said. 'I like the reading part best and I can do my sums. I've tried very hard,' he added with his head down.

Soon after her husband returned from Parliament Lady Grace spoke to him of Tony.

'He needs some guidance. He's been allowed to grow unchecked like wild vine. His size has made us think he was grown when in fact he's just a lonely boy,' she explained.

'I must admit that I've neglected my good intentions toward him,' Sir Beville admitted as he pulled at his pointed beard as if to bring some idea to mind. 'Yes,' he said thoughtfully, 'I think I shall train Tony as a soldier. He will have closer contact with people and he will be learning useful skills. When he's older he can teach them to others.'

So Tony moved into the big house, to a tiny room of his own in the attic. He ate with the servants of the house. During the day he worked with Davy, the groom, learning how to manage a horse. He practised the sword and musket which Sir Beville himself had taught him to use, and with his growing strength helped with the chores around the house.

His favourite time, however, was when Lady Grace would ask him to her sitting room to hear him read aloud. Sometimes he read a poem, sometimes some history. He learned about the Romans and King Arthur and his legends. He was curious and always wanted to know more.

It was reading that gave Tony the idea for the stories he made up as he sat in his room looking out over the valley and the far away farms. There was nothing of dreams down there, no far away places to be seen. Someday he would ride out and see things for himself.

Eating at the top end of the table with the household servants in the kitchen instead of with the garderners and grooms was strange at first. Lady Grace had instructed Cook to watch Tony's table manners which she interpreted in her own way. She sat with a large wooden spoon and for any grabbing or sloppiness he got a good thwack on the knuckles.

After the evening meals they would all sit by the fire like a big family with mending and talk of the day. Tony was self-appointed fire tender, poking and prodding it and always going for just a bit more wood. Cook and Dowlish the houseman were amused at how seriously he took this simple task. But in this way he at last felt he belonged.

Someone else watched him tend the fire. Sebella was tall and sturdy with a sweet face under brown curls peeping from under her linen cap. She always had a kind word for Tony as she sat with her mending by the fire. It was for her that he kept the fire warm but he wished he could think of something to say.

One day he had an idea. That evening he brought a book that he'd borrowed from Lady Grace. 'I could read to you a bit, if you want,' he offered.

'You're wonderful clever, Tony,' praised Sebella putting down her work to look at the book.

So Tony began reading aloud by the fire. Sir Beville was pleased at the change in his young giant in such a short space of time and made the library open to him, suggesting that he look at the maps and history books. He would be a good soldier someday, Sir Beville thought with pride.

CHAPTER 3
GENTLEMANLY SPORTS

The morning was chilly but the mist had lifted and it promised to be a beautiful day. Tony, now twenty three, rode proudly astride his great Blue Roan horse, watching a group of young boys as they rode along in front of him bouncing dutifully on their satin clad behinds. They were on a ride across the moor and on this spring morning it was all in bloom. The dark green gorse was covered in buttery yellow flowers while the blackthorn was all in white. Here and there a twisted oak, bent over by the wind, was purple with unopened buds.

They rode slowly along the natural paths between the low trees and patches of dry, copper coloured bracken. Although this was their favourite ride, today they were pleased when they came again in sight of Stowe. Sir Beville was coming home with news about the quarrel between the King and Parliament, gossip from the city and gifts for everyone.

Sir Beville himself rode out to meet their party. His wide lace collar flew back as he rode and a look of almost boyish happiness spread over his face as he saw his sons. He wore a wide brimmed hat, pinned up on one side, with a deep red plume in it. His ginger hair was neatly trimmed, stopping at his shoulders, and he had a pointed beard and moustache. Tony thought how proud he was to serve him.

Sir Beville Grenville, from his portrait

Sir Beville's interest in education had grown now that he had children of his own. He had invited his neighbours' sons to take advantage of the tutors he hired and Tony now instructed them in what Sir Beville called 'gentlemanly sports'. The high spirited boys needed a patient and kindly teacher who could keep up with them, hunting, fishing, fencing and playing ball.

Sir Beville had three sons and a daughter now: Dick, Beville, John and Bridget. Dick was thirteen and heir to the estate. He was a thin lad with a bad temper and a head for books rather than sports. He found the games they played on horseback tedious and exhausting and didn't mind saying so. Young Beville was seven, plump and good-natured but not strong. John, who was called Jack, was only five but already a good horseman. Little Bridget was three. But it was Dick who had all Sir Beville's attention.

'Boys! Tony!' he called as he rode towards them at a gallop. He stopped along side Tony and shook his hand. 'Well, how is he doing?' he asked, smiling at his eldest son.

'The boys are all doing very well, as you'll soon see, Sir,' Tony answered.

'You must come and see the new stallion I've brought,' Sir Beville said as he rode beside Dick. 'A real beauty. The darkest bay you can imagine.'

They rode back to the house in a holiday mood.

'Tony, you promised we would play soldiers today,' Jack reminded him as they dismounted. 'You promised.'

Tony had to smile as he looked down at the earnest little face. 'Now Master Jack, I don't think I quite promised for today.' He knelt beside the hopeful boys and put a great hand on each small shoulder. He was tired and there was still work to do. 'Master Bev has to go to his tutor now and Nurse is waiting for you with your sister. You wouldn't want Bridget to be lonely, would you?'

Jack shook his blond head with a disappointed frown. He did like playing with his three year old sister. She would do anything to please him and she was the only army Jack could command. But he liked playing soldiers with Tony better.

As they walked toward the house from the stables together Sir Beville said, 'Tony, the King has dissolved Parliament. He means to rule alone. There's talk in

London of fighting. I'm pleased with all you've done with the children, but now I have something more important for you to do. I'd like for you to join me and help train our local men as soldiers.

'Cornishmen must now be trained for fighting,' he continued. 'I have no idea how things will turn, but we must be prepared to defend Cornwall for the King if it should come to the worst. These will be difficult times and I will need your help.'

'I'm honoured, Sir,' Tony replied humbly. 'It's always been my dream to serve my King and country at your side.'

'Then it's settled,' Sir Beville smiled a tight smile and clasped Tony's hand with both of his.

Bev and Jack had been waiting at the house.

'Can we play soldiers, Tony?' Jack begged, looking hopefully from one man to the other.

'I think we can surely play soldiers today!' Tony laughed, bending down to lift them both up.

'Here!' their father cried in a rare, playful mood, 'here's a horse without a rider.'

'I'll ride Papa!' Bev cried running to his father who lifted him up onto his shoulders. And the little army was off.

'Make way for the Grenville Calvary!' Tony bellowed to announce them. 'Make way for the invincible Grenvilles!'

CHAPTER 4
BUTTERFLIES

Tony had just started down the back stairway from delivering Jack to the nursery when he heard a loud crash. He listened but there was no other sound. He walked back down the hall in the direction of the noise. Nurse looked out of the nursery, shrugged and went back to the children. At the far end of the hall in an unused bedroom he found Sebella sitting on the floor, rubbing her arm. A chair lay on its side beside her.

'Seb!' Tony cried in alarm. 'Are you hurt, girl?'

He went to help her up and saw there were tears in her eyes although she smiled at him. 'I'm not hurt, just feeling a bit foolish,' she replied. 'I was trying to reach some cobwebs and stretched too far. I didn't mean to frighten you.' She stood up and began brushing herself off, smoothing her skirt and straightening her cap. Tony thought how pretty she looked as she fussed.

'From now on,' he declared, pretending to be stern, 'Tony Payne will be the Duster of High Places. Is that understood, Miss?'

'You know I can't let the cobwebs hang about waiting for you to remember them,' she laughed at the idea. 'Well, maybe just the very high places, like that big tester bed.'

'I swear upon my honour not to neglect the high dusting of Sebella,' he declared holding the duster over his heart, 'if she'll remind me when it's needed.'

Tony was chuckling over his new chore as he started off down the hall but he was delayed once again by a call. 'Oh Tony, there you are!' Lady Grace and her sister and cousins from Stratton were just coming up the main stairway.

'Tony, the fabric has arrived for the dresses at last and is waiting to be unloaded from the coach. It needs a strong arm to bring it up,' she smiled up at him. 'The dressmaker is to have the small end bedroom and the room beside it to work. Please take the cloth in there, if you will.'

Tony frowned as he went down the stairs, hoping Seb had found all the cobwebs before she fell.

Lady Grace had had two babies in the last two years - George the year before and Roger just three months ago. Now she was having a new wardrobe made for herself. A seamstress from Exeter was coming to stay with drawings of the latest fashions and now Sir Beville's promised bolts of fabric from London had finally arrived. The ladies were in a spin of excitement.

The long rolls of cloth were carefully wrapped in protective linen. As each arrived upstairs, it was unwrapped and displayed. There was a pink satin brocade with dark, rose coloured blossoms and a creamy white one with gold spirals. There were soft woollens of burgundy and pearl grey and a shiny satins of crimson, cream and sky blue. The tiny room began to look like a garden in bloom with the seamstress, dressed in plain black and white, looking like a gardener with her scissors hanging by a ribbon from her waist.

Dressmaker's drawings c. 1630

As he watched he thought how pleasant it was to see the ladies bobbing about in their pretty gowns as they hurried to the table of drawings of the latest London dresses. They were like so many butterflies, he thought with a smile. He hardly dared to move in case he should step on their toes as they darted this way and that around the room.

He thought about Sebella and how pretty she looked in her simple clothes, going calmly about her work smelling like fresh air and lavender and never, never making a fuss. She was more of a bee than a butterfly, he decided.

When the last of the cloth was on the table, the door of the sewing room was closed for the ladies to be measured. Tony walked along the upstairs hall, looking out the window. Along a far lane Sebella was walking.

Tony hurried down the stairs and out of the house, galloping like a great horse across the field in order to reach the end of the lane and meet her as if by accident. At the hedge bordering the lane he found an opening and climbed down the steep grassy back onto the lane. The sunlight danced across the dusty stones in the path, dappling the dark nettles and fern-like bracken with yellow. Here and there a flower would shine in a tiny spot of light.

He thought how good it was to be out of the house and to smell the sweet grass and ploughed earth. The ladies were very beautiful but they smelled of heavy perfume. Tony liked the smells of baking and brewing that hung about the kitchen maids.

Sebella came around a bend. She was simply dressed in a grey wool skirt and a bodice that laced up the front. She broke into a broad smile at the sight of Tony.

'Right then?' he greeted her.

'Right then,' she replied.

Tony fell into step beside her and they continued in silence down the sunny lane. Sebella began picking buttercups and bluebells that popped out of the grassy bank. Some lacy angelica caught her eye and she reached into the long weeds to find its stem. With a sharp cry she pulled it out. She had put her hand into stinging nettles.

Tony found a dock leaf, broke it and rubbed it on her hand to soothe the sting. Then he reached into the weeds and plucked the flower for her. With a little bow he handed to her.

'Thank you, kind sir,' she said merrily.

With sudden playfulness he snapped off a piece of cleaver -'Sweet heart' they called it - a pale green weed with sticky hairs on its fat little leaves that stuck to whatever it touched. If it stuck to a girl, they said, she would be your sweetheart. Tony tossed it to Sebella. It stuck to her shoulder and she blushed, smiling as she picked it off and studied it. They walked together in contented silence.

Tony thought, I'll marry Seb one day for sure.

The following morning the boys had their riding and shooting practise, but Dick was no where to be found. Tony finished the class early and went to look for the boy. Sir Beville had been away in London for a long time and Dick had been especially difficult to teach.

It wasn't hard to guess where the missing Grenville might be. Tony went straight to the library.

The boy looked over the top of the book he was reading. 'You're supposed to be teaching shooting,' he said in a most superior manner. 'Do you think you may do as you please when my father is away?'

'Well, that seems to be much your way of looking at it,' Tony remarked evenly. 'Your father has told you that you must work at all your studies, not just the subjects that take your fancy. You must either do as your father says ... or explain to him why you don't want to continue some of them. It's time you talked to him about it and not just be sullen and miserable with me!' And with that he stormed out of the room.

Dick thought about this for some time. Sir Beville Genville had always seemed to give his son orders, never listening to him if he replied. No, he couldn't talk to his father at all. He went to find Tony and was told that he was upstairs - dusting a high tester bed.

Dick sat on the bed and watched curiously without speaking for a while. Tony hummed a little to fill the silence.

'Tony, there are all kinds things people become when they grow up. Why does my father think that I have to be a soldier? Can you see me riding around a field, shooting holes in men or cutting them open with a sword? I'd be hopeless.'

Tony looked down on the thin, spotty faced boy sitting miserably on the bed, a boy who loved poetry and history and who was already writing stories of his own. He could see that it wasn't the riding and shooting lessons Dick objected to, it was what they were to lead to in the future.

'You're the Grenville heir, Master Dick,' Tony reminded him kindly, 'and all the Grenvilles have been great soldiers. Then there's this great estate to run and all that governing at Parliament. All that takes a might of leadership. That's why you're father doesn't think about you being anything else.'

'But why can't Bev be the one who does all that instead? Maybe I'm like some other ancestors and not like an heir. I could be a clergyman or a tutor instead.' He looked earnestly up at the giant.

'I'm a-feared that the heir business has to go to the first born boy and there's no getting away from it,'

Tony smiled and put a reassuring hand on the boy's narrow shoulder. 'You're quite right that there are many ways to be a good man. You must explain this to your father. Show him the things you're good at, tell him how you don't want to learn to ride and shoot just to fight in battles.'

'Couldn't you talk to him for me, Tony?' Dick pleaded.

'No Master Dick, I'm afraid you're going to have to find the courage to do that yourself,' Tony said regretfully. He frowned as Dick slowly left the room, stooped and dragging his feet in a way that especially irritated his father. Maybe the giant could have a quiet word with Sir Beville.

'Oh Tony,' Dick hesitated in the doorway, 'I'm sorry they've made you do the dusting. You look really silly.' Then he went thoughtfully on his way. Tony burst into a great roar of laughter.

CHAPTER 5
A GLIMPSE OF HEAVEN

Sir Bernard Grenville was dead. The funeral procession stopped at the lych-gate and the coffin was carried in to rest between the two gates, one open to the outside street and the other closed to the churchyard until the vicar would let them in.

Tony had to stoop to get in but found head room under the open beams of the steep roof. It felt good to get in out of the drizzling rain. He suddenly sneezed and looked around shyly to see if anyone noticed but everyone had their head bowed.

The vicar came to meet them and made the sign of the cross before leading them slowly up the avenue of yew and ash trees to the doorway of the church and the beautiful stone arch another Grenville had had built a hundred years before. Beyond that was the

Norman archway built of stone brought all the way from France, Lady Grace had said.

Lychgate, Kilkhampton

The Grenvilles were a very old family. They could trace their ancestors back to Rollo, the first Duke of Normandy in the days of William the Conqueror. Generations of Grenvilles were buried here in the family tomb. It must be a comfort, Tony thought, to know where you would finally rest your bones, safe with your family.

The church smelled damp as they walked towards the Grenville Chapel at the front. All through the service Tony thought about families. He was now twenty six. It seemed he had always been part of the Grenville family and was proud of it.

As the mourners left the church, Jack fell into step beside him.

'Do you ever think about dying, Tony?' he asked with a frown. Jack was eight, serious and thoughtful.

'Not often, Master Jack,' Tony replied. 'Though in dark days like these it does pass through my mind now and again.'

'I shall be buried here one day, you know,' he continued, splashing through the puddles gently.

'Well, you don't seem any too pleased about it,' Tony commented, amused. 'I was thinking what a fine thing it is to have a family place in the church and how proud I'd be to be buried inside a church.'

'Still,' Jack said with a final sigh, 'it isn't better than being alive.'

'Good point, lad,' chuckled Tony at this philosophical comment.

It was after the months of mourning for Sir Bernard had passed that Sir Beville began to make preparations for Dick, now seventeen, to go to Oxford to college. He was to go to Gloucester College as his father had done and Sir Beville spent much of his time now writing letters to the headmaster concerning his son's education. And when he wasn't advising the headmaster, he was lecturing Dick on how important certain subjects were for a good education. He nagged about his son's posture, tried to explain about budgeting money, found more and more books that just had to be read before he went. Dick began hiding from his father whenever he saw him coming.

Tony loved to hear Sir Beville's stories of Oxford. He tried to imagine everyone in black robes and square hats looking as his master said, like a flock of crows in the streets and commons. He could hardly believe that the tutors and their students had once been fighting the townspeople, throwing things from the walls of the colleges. Perhaps Master Dick would have to learn to fight after all.

When the time came for Dick to leave and all his goodbyes were said, he and his father got into the carriage and drove off. As they stood waving on the drive everyone knew that Sir Beville had already started another lecture.

Lady Grace sighed, 'What a long journey it will be for poor Dick if his father gives him instruction all the way. Still, it wouldn't hurt him to listen once in a while.'

'Master Dick takes to books like a duck to water, my Lady. Not doubt he'll make his father proud.' Then Tony added timidly, 'He really isn't the sort to make a soldier.'

'That is true, but thank heaven for small mercies, Tony,' she said sadly. 'I couldn't bear to have all my family go to war. Will it really come to war, do you think? Or are these troublemakers just testing the strength of the King?'

If only it were that simple, Tony thought. The division between the King and Parliament was so great now that the country couldn't go in two directions. It seemed that only a fight could decide who would rule the country. But he said nothing to upset Lady Grace.

When Sir Beville returned from Oxford the two men returned to the army at Plymouth. Sir Beville worried constantly over Dick's progress. Did he study enough math or too much history? Why wasn't the headmaster reporting to him more often? Why didn't Dick answer his questions? And what was to be done about all Dick's overspending?

Finally Sir Beville lost patience. 'Go to Oxford and fetch him, Tony,' he ordered one day. 'I'll have him here. His laziness and extravagance are ruining me. Poetry! The army will teach him some discipline at least!'

When Tony returned with Dick, he took him to his father's office. Sir Beville was busy, worried and disappointed in his son.

'It's come to this. You've left me no choice,' he said crisply. 'You won't find my camp as comfortable or amusing as Oxford but I trust you will learn far more here. You will see me very little. Tony will look after you. Do you have anything to say?'

'Yes sir,' Dick stammered, 'I'm, well, very, um...'

'Sorry?' his father finished. 'I should think you are. Dismissed!'

Several weeks passed and Dick, like a prisoner doing his prison sentence, followed Tony's every command. It was many times more difficult than the games at Stowe and although he didn't complain he seemed to be getting even thinner. His every failure worried him until he began to look frightened and sad all the time. He had started to have a nervous twitch. Tony became deeply concerned about him and decided he must speak to Sir Beville.

'So you see, Sir, I don't think I should risk his health any further,' the giant concluded.

'I see, I see,' Sir Beville said with a resigned sigh. 'Tony, you know I'm only trying to do what's best for him. I believe your judgement about his health, but pushing him should make him stronger, more self-reliant. I want him to be a man!' He thumped the table in frustration.

The trouble between the King and Parliament had grown into a very complicated situation. The country became divided between those who supported the King and those who supported Parliament with both sides forming armies as war seemed to loom closer and closer.

The Grenvilles were a pious family. They were part of the Established Church and believed that God gave the King the right to rule. The King did what he felt was best for the country as directed by God. Being loyal to God meant being loyal to the King as well. They were Royalists.

However, the Parlimentarians saw things differently. They felt all people were equal under God's law and therefore a group elected by the people should decide what was best for the country. Their religion was woven together with their politics. Their dress was as simple as their prayers. Because the men cut their hair short, they were often called 'Roundheads'.

Tony knew the King had called for his supporters to raise troops in case there was an uprising. The country had no permanent army. Wealthy landowners recruited men, trained them and paid them with their own money. Now Sir Beville and his brother Richard were raising an army in Cornwall for the King. Silver and valuables were being collected to buy guns and powder.

It was Tony's duty to carry these to an underground passage leading from Stowe to Kilkhampton Church. When wagons arrived at night with arms, he unloaded them and stacked the guns away. The secret was important and Tony felt chills of excitement. It reminded him of his childhood games of smugglers on the beach.

To anyone visiting Stowe, the house would have seemed quite peaceful. The four youngest Grenville children played happily in the garden. The gardens and orchards blossomed and friends came and went.

It seemed much changed to Tony though. The boys of Sir Beville's academy had scattered to go to college or to join the army. Gentle Bev had recently died of small pox, Dick was at college and only Jack remained, studying with his tutors or riding alone on the moors.

One morning Tony thought he would take some time with Jack and ask him to go for a ride. He found the boy in the library, a partly drawn map in front of him on the table.

'Come in, Tony,' he smiled, putting down his pen. 'I'm drawing a map, a copy of this one. I thought it might be useful... in case.' The thought of war was on everyone's mind.

'Proper job!' Tony said admiringly. Jack was only thirteen and this work showed great skill and attention to valuable details.

'It's a fine day, Master Jack, would you care to ride with me?'

'I'd enjoy that,' Jack smiled up at him.

The November day was mild and sunny. They rode down through the orchards and along the stream towards the mill. They could see the tower of Kilkhampton church rising above the trees in the distance. Jack was silent as they rode, and Tony knew he had something on his mind.

'Father has sent for Dick to be with him and the regiment,' he said finally.

'That's so,' nodded Tony. 'And I suppose you know why he's done so?' He glanced at the boy beside him.

'I'm sure he thinks to make Dick a soldier,' Jack said flatly, his jealousy making him look very cross.

'Master Dick is there to learn discipline and mend his ways,' Tony said forcefully. 'He's too long been idle and studying such nonsense as your father never intended when he sent him off. He's spent far too much money and your father isn't pleased at all. He doesn't deserve to be envied, Master Jack.'

Jack felt better. They rode along, admiring the scenery. They paused to watch an otter dive into the water and saw a heron fishing.

'Do you think I might become a soldier?' Jack asked as they came in sight of the house again. 'Surely Father would be pleased about that.'

'Ah, Master Jack,' Tony sighed, understanding his feelings. 'Not for a few years yet. You keep your mind on your studies and that fine map copying for now.'

'I'll surely die of boredom while everyone else is having adventures!' he cried and spurred his horse to a gallop across the fallow field.

As they came to the house they saw a carriage and hurried to see who it was and with what news. It wasn't Sir Beville as they had half expected, but another Cavalier, dressed in purple satin and wearing a pistol at his belt. Tony recognised one of his 'young gentlemen', the Grenville's cousin, John Tremayne. He was helping a pale and weak young man from the carriage. It was Dick.

'What's happened to Master Dick?' Tony asked as Dick was helped inside the house by Dowlish.

'Tony, it's good to see you again.' The two men shook hands.

'I've brought my cousin home,' young Tremayne explained, 'and worse company I can't imagine, if you'll pardon my saying so. He hasn't exactly enjoyed his time with the regiment. His father sent him back with me as he appears to be ailing with something and I was coming home myself. This ailment may well be the result of his father's hard training, I fear. No doubt a soft bed and a good cup of wine will cure it shortly,' he laughed.

'Sir Beville requests that you see him safely back to Oxford when he's recovered,' he continued. 'There may be peaceful work for him yet. The King has recalled Parliament.'

As he watched the young man greet Jack and go into the house Tony felt a stab of disappointment. Yes, he knew how Jack felt about being left at home.

It was nearly two weeks before Dick was thought to be well enough to travel. As they set off he was actually smiling from his carriage. Tony rode beside him, glad for the chance to take a journey.

Oxford had impressed Tony. He was amazed by all the spires that seemed to crown the city. The many colleges, much like castles, could be seen only through their open gates. He hoped that he would have time to see a bit more on this visit.

Dick had told him much about his life at Oxford and especially the wonderful library which he described in great detail. When you entered the cobblestone courtyard there were tiny stone portrait heads on either side of each of the many heavy doors looking down on you as you entered. First you came into a grand hall and then you went up ramps and stairs to the reading room. It was called Duke Humphry's Reading Room, although Tony couldn't quite remember why.

The reading room had a coloured glass window at each end, as beautiful as any Tony could see in a church. The ceiling was vaulted, like a church as well, and painted with shields showing open books and family coats of arms. Rooms at the ends had shelves of books from floor to ceiling while the middle room was arranged in benches and desks for reading and writing.

Dick had told him about a bible he had been studying that had been written all by hand by monks who spent their days just copying books. The pages each had a large decorated first letter and many little drawing around the edges in blue, red and gold.

This was a different boy from the sullen lad who slouched in the saddle. His face was excited and happy when he was talking of things like this. Tony could understand a little better his misery at leaving such a peaceful place.

Duke Humphry's Reading Room

CHAPTER 6
THE HOLLY AND THE IVY

Winter's muted greens had settled over the fields of Stowe and the trees and hedges, now stripped of their leaves, looked like pen and ink sketches across the landscape.

It was Christmas 1640, but it wouldn't be the celebration it usually was. There would be no parties, no dancing, no house full of friends. The family were in mourning. Dick had died at Oxford shortly after Tony had left him. Tony liked to think of him there, peaceful in the library he loved so much.

For Sir Beville it was a terrible loss. He blamed himself first for not disciplining his son enough and then for being too hard on him. With the shock and grief of it he remembered his harsh words too clearly. He paced up and down the library, trying to decide what he should do. He couldn't afford an expensive Oxford education for Jack. All his money had been spent on raising an army and Dick's schooling. The family was deeply in debt. He would take Jack back with him for an education in the army.

Lady Grace still just sat, quiet and melancholy while the servants tried to keep the children from disturbing her. First Bev had died, then two of her babies and now Dick was gone as well. In those days children often died as babies or youngsters but it seemed impossible that some strange illness should have taken Dick. She couldn't think of anything but protecting all her family and keeping them close to her.

The house was too full of sadness, Tony thought. 'Here we come a-wassailing!' he sang as he walked out across the frozen fields. He would put himself in charge of keeping people happy, he decided. He turned and looked back at the house. It had started to rain. Surely it would snow in the night and transform everything into a bright and happy wonderland.

Tony entered the warm kitchen and rubbed his hands together by the fire. Young George and Roger played in front of it, burning twigs and leaves, berries and nuts to see what would happen. Holly and ivy popped and spat, brown ash and oak leaves left little white ghosts of themselves. Now the cat caught a mouse to the delight of the two boys and screams of the scullery maid.

By Christmas Eve, however, gloom had settled over the household. Jack and Bridget quarrelled, George and Roger were out of control and baby Jean whined and cried for her mother. Where are the carollers? Tony groaned. They would surely save the evening.

Every year carollers from the village came and sang to the family in the Great Hall with a lute and a tambourine to accompany them. The entire household joined in the singing and Lady Grace always said it was her favourite part of the holiday. Could they work their magic this year?

Tony began to be cheerful again. He thought of the bowl of hot wassail, ale and cider mixed with spices and Joe Skinner's secret ingredient. Everyone suspected that the gardener added some oranges to it but he would never admit to such extravagance. Little ginger cakes and mince meat tarts waited on platters for the singers and Tony's great belly began to growl with the thought of food.

The carollers arrived and arranged themselves in the Hall. The children sat on the floor and the servants crowded together at the door to the room. The Grenvilles greeted the singers and asked what news they brought. The singers then answered with the carol:

Masters in this hall, hear ye news today, Brought from overseas, and ever I you pray: Noel!

They sang all the favourites and as Tony looked around him it seemed like any other happy Christmas. But Lady Grace had quietly left the room.

When the carollers had gone the family moved into the cosier room next door and found Lady Grace sitting by the fire. Bridget ran to her, chattering about being allowed to strum several chords on the lute, while little Roger tried to drown her words by singing and clapping. Their mother looked patiently at her excited children and drew her shawl closer around her shoulders.

Lady Grace shivered and Sir Beville asked for another log to go on the fire. A maid in a starched white collar nodded and left the room.

'Nick,' she called from the door of the kitchen to the stable hand, 'her Ladyship needs more wood for the fire. She's rather poorly.'

Tony looked around at the family. They looked like a Puritan family in their sombre dark clothes. He wondered if Lady Grace would ever come out of mourning and have a new wardrobe again. It shouldn't be like this at Christmas, he thought. Where was that wood?

Sir Beville looked at Tony in such a helpless way that the giant got up and said, 'I'll just see what's keeping that wood, my Lady.'

Outside it was clear and cold. The stars twinkled and the air felt sharp. Halfway between the barn and the house, sitting on the ground was the scruffy Nick holding on to the lead of a donkey loaded with wood.

The more he tugged the more the donkey dug his hoofs into the ground.

'What in the world...?' Tony bellowed as he stood over the pathetic man. Nick looked terrified at the sight of the laughing giant above him. He dropped the rope and ran, then stumbled, then crawled into the darkness.

Tony had found his good spirits again. He picked up the donkey, logs and all, and went singing into the house.

'Make way! Make way!' he cried. 'Ass and fardel for my Lady's Yule, ass and fardel for my Lady's Yule!'

There were shrieks and shouts and the sound of a platter falling to the kitchen floor as he passed. Tony walked in and bowed to Lady Grace, still holding the frightened donkey and grinning impishly. Her mouth opened in disbelief. Sir Beville stood frozen like a statue, his pewter cup falling from his hand. Baby Jean ran to Bridget in fright. George and Roger danced with delight while Jack kept repeating, 'Oh Tony!'

Then from the startled lady came a sound they'd almost forgotten. Lady Grace was laughing.

Everyone clapped and the evening was saved. Tony began to sing in his rich bass voice and the others joined him.

The Holly and the Ivy
When they are both full grown
Of all the trees that are in the wood
The Holly bears the crown.

Oh, the rising of the sun
And the running of the deer
The playing of the merry organ
Sweet singing in the choir.

Tony looked around at the faces in the flickering fire light. The children came to sit quietly beside their mother. Sir Beville watched with a smile as she sat talking and stroking their heads.

Tony smiled to himself with satisfaction as he left the little donkey chewing a ginger cake in the warm barn.

Tony walked out into the night and looked up at the stars. Christmas brings such strange gifts, he thought with a smile.

CHAPTER 7
RUMBLINGS OF WAR

'Tony, a word,' Sir Beville said from the kitchen door. Tony had just carried a big cider barrel in for Cook's larder.

Tony wiped his hands and followed his master along the tiny passage ways to the room which Sir Beville kept as a study. The door of the room was barely big enough to the huge fellow to get through. Inside smelled of leather and pipe smoke. Maps lay on the desk and books from the library were stacked on a nearby chair.

'It will be war now, Tony,' Sir Beville began. 'There can be no other way to resolve these differences. The Parliamentarians are arming and we must defend our King and our faith. You're a good and trusted servant and have been with this family through many things. I rely on your loyalty and courage as much as I do your great strength. Now I need all of these qualities. Tony will you fight beside me as my body guard?'

'It would be a proud honour, Sir,' Tony replied at once. The two men shook hands and Sir Beville poured wine to drink to their future and to the King.

'We'll leave as soon as I've arranged things here. I want to take young Jack with me so he can continue with your fine instruction,' Sir Beville smiled. 'Now, if you'll excuse me, I must try to break this news to his mother!'

A frozen fog had settled over the fields and as she sat with her needlework Lady Grace could barely see beyond the front gardens. It was as if the world ended at the hedge. She tried to imagine the summer warmth as she worked delicate violets in tiny stitches on a piece of linen stretched tight by her round embroidery hoop. The breezes came off the ocean in summer and she could imagine the children playing in the garden below in the summer violets. She got up and opened the window to smell the flowers.

'Grace!' Sir Beville cried as he entered the room. 'For Heaven's sake, you'll catch your death of the cold!' He closed the window and sat in the chair beside his wife looking into her face.

'I don't know what came over me,' she said, bewildered. 'It was the flowers, I suppose.' Still looking puzzled, she took up her embroidery again.

Sir Beville gave his wife a worried look. She certainly wasn't herself these days. He gave a nervous little cough.

'I've been thinking of young Jack's education,' he began. 'His tutors have given him the treasures of their minds, the gems of wisdom from ages gone by...' He made a wide gesture with his hand, trying to think how to say what he'd come to say.

'I quite agree,' said his wife without looking up. 'I can see that Jack could do with a change now.'

'I'm so glad you agree, my dear,' he sighed with relief.

'Yes, I was going to suggest that you find him a suitable art master this spring. He does so love to draw.'

'An art master!' Sir Beville stared at his wife in disbelief and then tried to calm his voice. 'I am referring to the boy's proper education, Grace. There is no money left for him. These are very hard times for us.'

'I had no idea,' she said with feeling. 'I do understand now.'

'I've given this much thought and I think I have found a solution. Jack will accompany me to Plymouth and be educated as a soldier.'

Lady Grace stood and stared at her husband, opened her mouth to speak and then fainted.

Sir Beville agreed to postpone Jack's leaving until the following year. After all, as his wife had reasoned, the boy was only thirteen. The country was on the verge of war and he could understand Lady Grace's fear for Jack's life. But mostly he was a loving husband and couldn't bear to give his wife any more unhappiness.

Meanwhile Tony went out to the stables and saddled his grey shire horse. His mind was on Sebella and how she would take his news. She now had duties at Houndapit, where the master's hunting hounds were kept. The road was steep or the happy giant would have had a good gallop.

As he drew up in the enclosed courtyard he could hear the hounds baying behind the house. He tied his horse and went to the kitchen door.

'Good day, Tony,' Sebella said cheerfully as she opened the door. 'Did you come to see Master Dawe? He's with the hounds.'

'Truth is Seb, I've come to see you, to say goodbye. I'm leaving with Sir Beville to serve as his body guard,' he added hoping that she would be impressed.

Sebella looked at him in amazement. She had always thought of him as a quiet, kindly fellow, quite different to her idea of a soldier. She was very fond of him and he could be hurt or even killed if the war began.

'Surely there's no fighting. Why then does the master need a body guard?' she asked suspiciously.

Tony realised that he shouldn't tell her too much. It wouldn't do for it to be known that they were secretly collecting money and buying arms to store at Stowe.

'Oh I'll just be helping to train men and carry messages,' he passed the job off lightly, although it hurt his pride to do so. 'I don't reckon I'll be away long. You know how these things have always passed.'

This didn't sound dangerous and Sebella felt better. 'Good. Then take care of yourself Tony, I shall miss you.'

They left Stowe without Jack and with none of the usual family farewells. Lady Grace sent a letter soon after asking her husband to forgive her as she was still upset about Dick's death.

Life at camp was full of activity. News from London reached them daily and Tony felt the excitement he had missed in the quiet and isolated life at Stowe. He travelled from village to village, recruiting men and raising money to buy arms. The guns were taken on secret trips to Stowe to hide in the ancient tunnel between the house and the church.

It was two years after Tony left Stowe that the call to arms finally came. Nothing in his world would be the same again.

Sir Beville wrote to his wife, advising her to pack the family and be ready to move into the manor at

Stratton, near her sister. Stowe was too isolated and too dangerous with its secret stores. Tony would be in charge of seeing them safely away and would close up the house. Master Jack would be coming back with him to join the army at last.

Actually Tony had another important job to do. As soon as the family were gone he was to blow up the secret passage half way along and cover the opening in the cellar. All valuables and anything useful to the enemy were to be disposed of or hidden. Hereafter the access to the stores would be through the church. The Grenville crypt held the other entrance and since the stone had been disturbed for Dick's burial their activities wouldn't be noticed.

The move from Stowe was easier than Tony had imagined. Of course everything of value had been given to raise money for the cause, even the lovely tapestries. He felt a great sadness as he walked through the empty house. The land had been mortgaged and Tony wondered what would become of Sir Beville's pears and apples. He looked out a window at the fish ponds in the garden built centuries earlier and wondered if they had ever seen such hard times.

Now he called to Jack to help him set up the powder in the passage below. It would be his first assignment for the King. They lit the fuses one after another until the tunnel was blocked all the way to the cellar door. Shelves and empty barrels were put in front of it so no one would notice. Just then they heard the sound of footsteps above, the quiet careful steps of a thief or an enemy spy.

Tony drew his sword and signalled Jack to do the same. Quietly they moved up the stairs and were just in time to see a ragged man running out. They let him go. Things were hard for the people around and the house would soon be safely locked up.

They would look in at Houndapit and Kespit, where the falcons were kept, to see that all was well. Sir Beville still looked after a few faithful servants there and Tony must give them some provisions. Tony knew that Sebella was still at Houndapit but because of the secret nature of his visits he'd not seen her in a year.

'Seb!' Tony called as he dismounted in the courtyard. Sebella had stayed here to look after the old cook and Dawe. He walked up and knocked on the kitchen door but got no answer. He went to the back where he found her, thin and tired, feeding moulding bread to two dogs.

'Seb, are you all right?' He went to her. 'Where is Dawe and old Cook?'

'Tony, you do look fine,' she smiled up at him. 'Dawe died last winter and then Nick came and said he had no work so he's here. Cook is poorly but she never complains. We thought you'd forgotten us. We never see anyone from the big house.'

'My dear soul!' Tony exclaimed. 'The master left word you were to be kept in provisions.'

'All the farm workers have gone off. There's no crops planted and there wasn't much of a harvest. Those that are left work with such a half will that nothing gets done. We've got a little garden patch so we make do,' she looked at the ground.

'And Nick's quite peculiar now,' she continued. 'He has a bad temper and it frightens me. He has strange friends and keeps even stranger hours. I can't think what he might be getting up to.'

She put her face into her hands and began to cry softly. Tony awkwardly put an arm around her for comfort.

'Seb,' he said quietly, 'I know this is an odd time to ask, but I've only just got up my courage. Will you be my wife, Seb? I always had it in my mind that we'd be married but I never figured how to ask.'

'Tony, I was afraid you were never going to ask,' she smiled a smile that said everything.

'I'm moving you and Cook into Stratton with Lady Grace and the children. You'll be safe and well cared for there. She's rather poorly you know and could use more help,' he said with authority. 'Nick had better be found in case he's up to some mischief.' He was thinking of how much Nick might have known of the arms stores.

He had no trouble persuading kind Lady Grace to employ Sebella at Stratton. She knew the woman was loyal and was pleased that Tony was at last going to take a wife. What a strange moment to pick to ask her, though. The couple would be married when Tony was next given leave and Sebella was back to good health, she decided, and wrote to her husband immediately.

It was time to leave. Tony went to fetch Jack and found Lady Grace pale and worried and even her brave smile couldn't hide her sadness.

'I'm sorry to take him away from you, my Lady,' he began helplessly.

'It's all right, Tony,' she smiled at the huge man on his knee before her chair. 'Only promise to bring him back to me.' She looked so tiny and so brave. It occurred to him that the King would never know how many wives and mothers were giving their dearest treasures, their families, to his cause.

'You can count on me while there's a breath in my body,' he answered sincerely.

Tony found Jack in the study rolling up another map he'd drawn.

'Are we leaving now?' he asked excitedly, 'I've been drawing maps so I can understand the battle plans.'

'Your father will be pleased, Master Jack.'

Everything was ready to leave. Goodbyes were so difficult and he'd been thinking what to say to Seb all night.

'Goodbye, Tony. God keep you safe,' she said holding both his hands.

'I'll write to you,' he said, imitating what Sir Beville always said to Lady Grace.

From her pocket Seb took a little crucifix. It had been her mother's. 'Keep this until you're home safe,' she said, pressing it into his big hand. He kissed her on the forehead and joined the men and horses waiting for them in the courtyard.

Jack stepped from the hall where he had been saying goodbye to his mother. He had waited so long for this time to come that it was hard to act sad at leaving. He looked like a prince in burgundy satin with his blond hair flowing to his shoulders. A sword hung at his side and he carried a black hat trimmed with a golden plume. Lace hung from his wrists and at his throat and like the other Cavaliers, he appeared to be going to a ball rather than to a war. A party of five guards from Stratton in their less decorative uniforms were to escort them.

A Chavalier and one of 'Waller's Lobsters'

The gates of Stratton Manor opened onto the main street of town and Tony was amazed to see the crowd of townspeople lined up to wish them well. Lady Grace and the household stood in doorways and windows waving. Tony looked around for Sebella. Jack tapped his arm and pointed above him and as he looked up flower petals fell down on him.

'You old Devil,' Jack chuckled merrily.

CHAPTER 8
SPOOF AND MOULD ALE

Tony was back in Stratton. He'd left no more than a few months ago, thinking it would be years before he saw it again. Well, he thought, you just never know.

It was a warm summer evening - warmer than most - and the air smelled of jasmine and roses. Stratton shimmered with heat rising from the cobblestone. Open windows in all the houses filled the streets with the smells of cooking. Children laughed and called as they ran barefooted down the hill past the gates of the Grenville manor house.

It was different this time. Sir Beville, Sir Richard and Jack were here and one hundred men besides. Each town in North Cornwall was to have a platoon of a hundred men, given room and food by the townspeople. General Stamford's Roundheads were on the march to fight the King's men for Cornwall. There was talk that the Roundheads had some new armour that made them invincible - 'Lobsters' they called them. Sorry talk indeed!

Tonight all this talk of war and enemies, noise and smoke seemed like a bad dream. Tony was restless and uncomfortably warm. The Grenville house was overcrowded with family and he hadn't had much time to see Sebella as she was always busy. There hadn't been time to be married yet and Sir Beville thought it would be best to wait until things were peaceful again.

He tried to hide his sour feelings. He opened the door in the oak gates and stepped out. Looking up the street he saw the Butcher's Arms and remembered the days when he'd sat at the long trestle table on market day, eating and talking with the farmers. Those were days when he was going to be a gardener, doing nothing more exciting than fighting curly leaf and mealy bugs.

Now he walked toward the inn and turned under the arch of the coach entrance. He had to stoop to get into the tiny square room of the public house. He sometimes wondered how small people must have been when this old inn was built! He found a place on the bench that ran all around the room. Soldiers laughed and talked and drank from pewter tankards.

'Master Blatchford!' Tony called as the innkeeper recognised him. 'Give us a tankard, will you?'

The round, bald headed man disappeared through a door into a room nearly as big as the first full of big barrels of ale. From a large pitcher he poured ale into a tankard and brought it to Tony.

'It's good to see you, Tony Payne!' Blatchford said. 'What's this I hear about you getting married? Must be nice being such good friends with Sir Beville. Guess you won't have any money problems. Nice to see you.' And with that he hurried off to serve another soldier.

Tony chuckled. He had forgotten how it was when you lived in a village and everyone knew your business and even some you didn't know yet! He closed his eyes and took a long swallow of the cool, bitter ale. With a sigh of satisfaction he set his nearly empty pot down on the table and turned his attention to games.

Beside him two fellows were playing 'snake eyes'. A wooden tray about a foot long was passed from one to another. Along one side was a row of nine wooden compartments, each with a slide to cover the numbers from one to nine printed on the bottom. A player rolled a pair of dice and covered the boxes with those numbers until he rolled numbers he couldn't use. The one with the most boxes covered was the winner.

The box came to Tony. He rolled the dice into the open area, bouncing them nicely off the side. Three and five. He added them and covered eight. Double fives. He could divide this into four and six. Soon he had covered all but the one. He shook a single die. Three! No good. His score was one. The next player would have to cover all the boxes to beat it.

Across the room, several men stood with a bull ring that hung by a rope from the ceiling. They took turns swinging it to see who could hang it on the meat hook on the opposite wall.

Tony could hear the sound of coins dropping on the floor. Plink, plunk. Some of the men had started a penny pitch, using Tony's boot and the mark. The man who came closest to the giant's boot without touching it picked up all the coins.

'Seven!' came a call from another corner.

'Ten!' someone else replied.

'Nine!' said another.

They were playing 'spoof'. Each man held a fist forward with from zero to three coins in it. They took turns guessing the number they held all together. The man who guessed closest dropped out.

Gradually the talk turned to war and politics. Games were laid aside and Tony felt restless again. There was no getting away from it - stories of the recent battles, Cromwell's latest decrees, the King's troubles, the hard times. Tony wished for the days when they told ridiculous tall tales or guessed at riddles. He sat playing snake eyes by himself.

But just then, through the open door to the stable yard came music. Four musicians had arranged themselves outside and were starting to play. One man played a lute, another a mandolin. A Cavalier in faded finery beat a bodhran while a frail little lady blew on a tin whistle. As they began to play, Tony leaned against a wall outside, tapping his foot. They played jigs and love songs, Celtic ballads and hymns.

The woman put down her whistle and sang in a high reedy voice that floated through the night. She rocked back and forth as she sang, closing her eyes. They should have more music around in these sad times, Tony thought. He looked at the thoughtful, relaxed faces of the soldiers. It took them away from their worries. He thought of Sebella, near to him and safe and soon to be his wife.

The music ended and the smiling soldiers, some with sentimental tears in their eyes, put coins into the old Cavalier's hat as he passed it around. Blatchford bid his guests God's speed and everyone made their way towards their beds.

Tony went up through the town and sat in the churchyard on a little knoll. He stretched his long arms and arched his tired back. The stars sparkled like pinpricks in the velvet cloak of heaven, he thought poetically, letting through the light beyond. The church bell tolled the curfew and the soft-hearted giant took a deep breath of the night air before making his way home.

CHAPTER 9
A GRENVILLE LEADS YOU STILL!

There was an eerie hush over the valley before them. Below, the River Neete flowed snakelike between the fields where sheep grazed peacefully. Something about this view from Stamford Hill made Tony think of the Twenty-third Psalm. 'Yea, though I walk through the valley of the shadow of Death, I will fear no Evil,' he repeated to himself.

As he looked over the troops assembled he could hardly imagine them as they were only a few nights ago at the Butcher's Arms. These men looked hard and ready as any fighting men, he thought proudly.

And then the enemy came. Tony could hardly remember it afterward. There were troops in neat rows and then the next moment there was noise and smoke and blood. And then suddenly they knew they had won. The feeling was wonderful.

But then the giant began to look around and take in the scene. There were human beings all over the ground, some dead, some wounded, some crying. He felt sick at heart as he began to look for the wounded.

Jack hadn't fought in the battle. On his father's orders he could only watch. He must see what acts were foolish and which were brave. The boy looked sad and serious as he helped to count the casualties.

They began to bury the dead, eight bodies to a grave. When they were nearly finished, and as Tony was making his last trip to the final grave with two bodies a voice from under his arm called, 'Oh please, no!'

Tony dropped the bodies in utter terror. He was tired, thirsty, superstitious and ready to believe in ghosts. He wanted to run but his feet didn't move.

'Don't bury me alive,' the body on the ground pleaded. 'You're the Giant. They said you eat prisoners. I was so afraid of you I pretended to be dead, then I passed out. Have mercy!'

'Well, my dear soul!' the giant exclaimed. He gently lifted the man to his feet, but he collapsed in pain.

'A broken leg,' Tony said. 'You'll mend.' He carried the Roundhead to the wagon for the wounded prisoners. Eating prisoners! What would they say next about the Giant of Stratton.

Grenville's army pressed on toward Bath. The enemy was on the run and Sir Beville thought he could finish the Roundhead's western army. News had come that General Waller's New Army was being sent to meet them. Waller had fresh troops and a new armour which nearly covered the men completely. "Waller's lobsters" they called them.

Grenville moved his men on until they met Waller at Lansdowne Hill, just above Bath. Sir Beville and

Waller had once been friends and it made the good man sad to think of fighting him. Now Waller had the important advantage of being up the hill. It would be difficult to fight them from below.

Sir Beville decided to attack anyway, his gunners firing the awkward wheel lock guns, backed up by cannons, but they were in a poor position. Grenville saw that they must change their position and ordered a retreat to Marshfield nearby.

Luck was with them. The Roundheads mistook this as a sign of the Royalists' defeat and down they poured from the safety of the hill. The Cornish horses and infantry turned and the battle raged back up the hill, with a sure victory in sight for Sir Beville's men.

They were running out of powder as they reached the top of the hill. Sir Beville sent the men with long pikes forward to hide this, but the hill was too dark with smoke to see anything.

Tony stood with Sir Beville and Jack on top of a house to get a better look at the battle and find the enemy for a last victorious charge. The general was sure of his men and his cause. 'You both will ride beside me,' he smiled.

The sound of clashing metal was deafening and Tony could hardly breath for the stinging smoke. He lashed out at the enemy as they rushed into the fighting. But suddenly there was a gasp beside him. Sir Beville fell to the ground, a pike through his chest.

It was a death blow and his men saw it. They started to fall back and look bewildered. Tony was torn between wanting to carry his master off and knowing that the battle would be lost if he did, and carrying on the fight.

Something from the past brought him into action. It was the ancient Grenville battle cry from long ago. It had stirred men then and it could unite them now.

'A Grenville leads you still!' he cried, and pulling Jack over onto his father's horse, Tony led the men forward. 'A Grenville leads you still!'

The men picked up their weapons. From all over the field came the cry, 'A Grenville, a Grenville leads us still!'

Choking back tears, Tony and Jack led the shouting men to victory. Jack would later have the title, Viscount of Lansdowne and Sir Beville, even after his death, would be the Earl of Bath to mark their victory that day.

At camp, Tony got ready to take Sir Beville's body back to Kilkhampton for burial. It would be a slow and sad trip. He decided to send a letter on ahead to Lady Grace so that she would know the news before she heard it from gossip. He wanted to tell her what he would never be able to say to her in person. As he wrote he could see her brave and tear streaked face.

He wrote:

Dear Honoured Madam,

Bad news flies fast and no doubt the heavy tidings have already reached that we have lost our master. You must not, dear lady, grieve too much for your husband. You know, as we all do, that his soul was in Heaven before his bones were cold. He fell as he often told us he wished to die, in the great Stuart cause, for his country and his king.

Master Jack, when I mounted him on his father's horse, rode into the war like a young prince, and our men followed him with their swords drawn and with tears in their eyes. They said they would kill a rebel for every hair in Sir Beville's beard, but I bade them remember their good master's words when he wiped his sword after the Stamford fight, when they said, 'Stab and slay!' 'Halt men,' he said, 'God will avenge.'

I am coming down with the most mournful load that ever a poor servant could bear, to bring that great heart to Kilkhampton vault. Oh, my lady, how shall I look into your weeping face?

These, honoured madam, from your servant

Antony Payne

It was indeed too much for Lady Grace to bear. She was too frail with all the hardships of war and went into decline. She died four years after her husband.

The great victory of Lansdowne faded as the war dragged on. Tony could hardly believe the news of defeats and losses of Sir Richard's men. He only wanted to go home. He felt tired and sick of all the fighting.

Then came the news: King Charles had been executed by the new Lord Protector, Oliver Cromwell. The King's son, Charles, had fled the country. They all were wanted men and would surely be executed, so the Royalist soldiers ran, each his own way.

Tony started for Stowe with Jack and a few loyal men. There would be places to hide, he thought. Suddenly ahead a man leapt into the road. Tony drew his sword, and then recognising him as Harry, a fellow soldier, and pulled up his horse.

'Sir Richard has fled and sends me to warn you that Stowe isn't safe,' he said. 'I have a safe house for you to rest. Sir John, we have plans to get you out of the country tonight.'

It made Tony start to hear his master addressed like this. He was no longer a boy but a hero and a fugitive, like the King. Harry led them through the orchards away from Stowe. The house stood quiet, still closed and empty. The orchards were overgrown with weeds and young trees so that you would hardly know they had been there. They walked the horses quietly until they came to the river.

The miller hid them in his mill for the night. Tony and Jack lay among the sacks of grain and slept immediately.

Then there was a noise. Tony opened his eyes. It was dark and he felt bruised and stiff and very hungry. 'Tony, Tony!' Jack was saying quietly, shaking his shoulder. The Miller appeared with bread and ale. Harry followed.

'It was the best I could do,' he apologised as he offered it.

'We have a good distance to cover to meet the boats,' Harry explained. 'They'll surely be watching Duckpool tonight so we're to go north.'

They rode in an old wagon, it's sides rotten and clattering. They were under blankets between some firewood. Harry sat slumped over the reins like a tired peasant as he drove the miserable bony horse through the cold drizzling rain. There were so many hills and sharp turns that his eyes were constantly watching for danger.

At Morwenstowe Harry turned the wagon towards the Bush Inn, drove past it and down a path into the woods. He got down and led the horse across a stream and up a steep path made up with cobbles and ridged with logs so the smugglers' wagons could safely carry their heavy loads from the sea to the Bush. He stopped at the edge of the woody cover. Beyond was an open valley leading to the sea.

'You'll have to walk now. They're waiting for you in the smugglers' cove beyond Sharpnose Point. God speed you both!' And with that Harry disappeared.

They made their way across the meadow and up the steep cliff path. Just when Tony felt he couldn't go any further they reached to top and there below was the wide grassy path curving down to the cove and the boats waiting. He felt like crying he was so thankful.

Then they were on the water and away, just as the first orange of daybreak appeared on the ripples. Their victory, their defeat had all passed so quickly. He wondered where this journey would take him, when he could ever come back and when he would ever see Sebella again.

CHAPTER 10
PORTRAIT OF A GIANT

King Charles was beheaded in 1649 and Oliver Cromwell ruled the country with Parliament as the Lord Protector. Many years later, after the death of Cromwell and much debate, Parliament invited the heir to the throne to come back. It was Sir John Grenville who presented the letter from Charles to Parliament, accepting their invitation to return and on 25 May 1660 he landed at Dover and was crowned King Charles II.

The new King had rewarded all his faithful friends who had offered their money and lives for him. Jack, now Earl of Bath, had been made governor of Plymouth and Tony a Yeoman of the Guards and Harbinger of the Arms. As a gift for all the Grenville sacrifices the King had promised a new house at Stowe. For Tony there was still another surprise.

'Tony!' Jack called from the Armoury window to the passing giant. His voice had the sound of a command in it.

'Yes, sir,' Tony said as he entered the sunny hall, lined with guns and cannon.

'This is Mr Kneller, Tony,' Jack introduced the stranger standing beside him. 'It seems that His Majesty would like to have your portrait painted and has sent Mr Kneller to do it. I leave it to you gentlemen to make the arrangements for the sittings. Please excuse me.' And with that Jack left the room before he burst out laughing. The look of surprise on Tony's face was just too funny.

Tony was both embarrassed and pleased. He had admired all the Grenville family portraits. It was as if you could know someone from a hundred years ago. He could hardly believe that it was the King himself who had commissioned it. He went red with pride.

Mr Kneller stood stiffly in front of Tony, wondering what to say. In one hand he held the handle of a small case which held his paints and in the other, clasped under his arm he carried a package wrapped in brown paper. He was looking at the biggest man he had ever seen and he hoped with all his might that he was friendly.

'I must measure you, Sir,' he said finally. 'The King has said that I must paint you life size.' The painter was shorter than most men and rather thin. He had sandy hair and bright blue eyes with merry crinkle lines about his face. He wore small gold rimmed spectacles that sat like a pair of windows somewhere between his eyes and the end of his nose. Tony wondered how they stayed there.

Suddenly the little man began to pace up and down, muttering to himself looking from time to time towards Tony. He stepped back and put up his thumb, measuring all the way to the giant's boots with little jabs at the air. 'Perfect!' he pronounced.

Tony had grown tired of standing and leaned back to rest against a cannon. He thought they were off to a good start if the painter thought him 'perfect' but he couldn't make out what the man's strange gestures meant. Now he was looking here and there and out the window, searching for something. Then his eyes fell on Tony.

'You are a genius, Sir!' he cried happily. 'That's it - beside the cannon! I like my subjects to feel at ease. Shall we begin tomorrow morning at nine?' And abruptly he picked up his belongings and was gone.

Jack came to find out how the interview had gone.

'I must say, Tony,' he smiled as Tony poured them each a tankard of cider from his private supply. 'You certainly have made a name for yourself. Imagine a full sized portrait. It'll take enough canvas to rig a ship, I swear.'

Tony turned red again and looked at the floor.

'You know I'm pleased for you,' Jack said quickly, seeing that Tony was feeling shy about the painting. 'It'll be a magnificent portrait! You must promise to wear your best collar and wash your hair.' Jack fussed.

'I'm thinking this portrait business may be more of a bother than I thought,' Tony laughed.

The painter was a person who could make you feel you had known him for ages and Tony enjoyed their chats as much as he did watching him draw.

Tony, from his portratit

First Mr Kneller drew the giant's face and hands from all directions. He worked with a stick of charcoal on sheets of paper tinted with light brown ink. Tony was amazed to watch how the simple lines were smudged to make rounded shadows and how white chalk on the places the light fell make everything seem to stand out and become real. Mr Kneller was so pleased at his interest that he let him try his hand at it.

A wooden support had to be built and canvas stretched tight over it. Mr Kneller's assistants covered it with many layers of horse glue and then sanded it smooth. When the painter was satisfied with the canvas he began to paint, first only like a drawing then with more and more colour. Drawings of Tony were all over the room he'd been given as a studio. Tony didn't have to pose every day now but he often looked in to see how things were coming along.

Jack was excited about the new house. Sir Beville had mortgaged all his property and sold his valuables to pay for guns and soldiers. Now Jack spent hours working on the plans, talking with the architect who had built the Citedel in Plymouth and drawing plans himself in fine ink lines with tiny lettering. Tony remembered the boy and his maps before the war. He had been happy about the new house until he heard that the old house was to be pulled down.

'That house has been there for hundreds of years,' Tony protested. 'You could add wonderful things to it, but why tear it down?'

'You're talking like an old man,' Jack smiled. 'That's just why the old house is going. Remember how damp and cold it was? Do you remember how small the rooms were? There's nothing wrong with having a new stylish house. You never know, I might have hundred's of children and need the space!'

Like the King, Jack had married after his return from exile. He already had children and he wanted to be sure they would have a fine home for the future.

Jack laughed and made a joke of it all, but there was much more in his mind than he said to Tony. There was nothing wrong with change, he thought, that was what life was all about. He was a favourite of the King who was taking a personal interest in this new Stowe house. No doubt he and the court would visit the Grenville's when it was finished. Jack smiled and added a flourish to the already ornate design of the front.

Tony left Jack with a feeling of sadness something like homesickness. He was thinking of change as well and realised that now Master Jack was Sir John his days of watching over him and advising him were over. He felt as if he had lost his family, and now they would pull down the house that had been a home to him.

He thought of this until he became tired and quiet with the unhappiness. At last he went to the stables, saddled his horse and rode out into the open countryside. Jack was too preoccupied with his house plans to notice but the observant artist watched the giant thunder out on his great steed. With sudden inspiration he picked up his brush and with a few strokes painted a hint of sadness in the giant's eyes.

CHAPTER 11
THE KING IS AMUSED

A grey haired Antony Payne stood on the cliff at Stowe looking out at the sea. Beside him a pair of small boys stood, impatient to be doing something more interesting than watching the waves on the rocks below. They tugged at his coat several times before he noticed them.

Tony looked fondly down at his young charges and smiled. Little Johnny Grenville was only five but as serious and quiet as his father had been. Charlie was now nine and already a good horseman.

'Come along then,' the giant said, bending down to pick the boys up on his shoulders. He was happy again, teaching the boys all the things he'd taught their father and uncles so long ago. Although he was now sixty, he hadn't felt so young in years.

From her window Lady Jane Grenville watched him galloping with the boys towards the house. She frowned. Hadn't she told her husband that Tony shouldn't be allowed to carry the boys like that at his age. She had always been a little afraid of Tony and spoke to him as little as possible. Secretly she wished Tony could be sent away and so was always pointing out his faults to her husband.

But Jack was never critical of his old friend. Although he had little time to talk with Tony, Jack liked having him about, telling the boys stories of the old days. He was the grandfather they didn't have.

Spring was coming. Snowdrops and daffodils were dying back. Bluebells were sprouting from the cold wet clay in the dells and the orchards were covered with fat purple buds. The boys had found frog spawn in the pond and everyone agreed that there had been some very mild days just lately.

Lady Jane sat at her little desk, writing. As usual, her husband was in London and she was sending him their news. The steward knocked at the door.

'My lady, a letter,' he announced, proudly handing her a small envelope bearing the royal seal.

Lady Jane trembled as she opened it and read the message penned on parchment. His Majesty the King would be pleased to visit the new house at Stowe during his tour of Cornwall the following month.

The Great House at Stowe, from an etching

'See to his Majesty's courier while I write a reply,' she said as calmly as she could. When the steward had left the room she began to laugh. Her heart was pounding with excitement over the royal visit and all it could mean for her family. She had been a lady in waiting to the queen before she had children and she missed the busy life of court. She thought of the ball gowns and palace rooms sparkling with crystal chandeliers, the beautiful and interesting company, as well as the wicked gossip. This would be an excellent opportunity to present her daughters, Jane and Grace, still in their mid teens.

She began organising it all in her mind at once. There were so many preparations to make and so little time to do them. She would have the latest designs for the gardens. Some extra men would have to be hired. There should be a French cook to supervise the kitchen as the King had become very fond of French food while he was in France. It would be expensive, but they didn't want to look like country bumpkins. They must have new clothes and the King's chambers would be specially decorated.

The sensible thing, she decided, was to make a visit herself to London to catch up on all new trends and the latest topics of conversation. She could hire a French cook and a good dressmaker at the same time. The girls would go with her.

Dressmaker's drawings c. 1665

She carefully wrote that the Grenvilles would be honoured to receive His Majesty, closed the envelope and heated the sealing wax. Into the little blob of wax on the flap she pressed her husband's seal, then hurried to give the Steward her reply.

The trip to London was a great success. Lady Jane returned with a set of sketches of the most talked about gardens, a rather haughty but well-trained cook and a sour-faced, bony seamstress who could not only reproduce the latest Paris fashions but teach the girls French as well. Lady Jane reasoned that as she had saved the cost of a gardener - the men could work from the sketches - she could afford three new dresses for herself. Soon the household was in utter chaos.

'A man could fine more peace on a battle field than he could in a house of agitated women!' Tony grumbled.

In the kitchen Polly the old cook was fuming about the new French cooking.

'Ruined a good joint of meat with her fancy ways. It smelled worse than I can tell you with that garlic. She just can't let anything alone. It's sauces with everything. I won't feel right serving up food what's been done all peculiar to England's own King,' she sulked, her face red and her fat arms folded across her heaving chest.

The dressmaker turned out to be happier teaching French to the girls than making dresses and if Lady Jane hadn't brought in several seamstresses from Exeter there would have been no new gowns at all.

The gardeners were puzzled by the drawings which were their only instructions. There was nothing about what plants had been used for the borders of the tight geometrical flower beds and no notes as to which were flowers and which were shrubs within. None of the gardens Lady Jane had seen had been in bloom yet. In the end it looked nothing like what Lady Jane had wanted but she sighed and said it would have to do as there was no more time.

With everyone doing their best Stowe was finally ready to receive the King. The day was mild and a gentle breeze wafted scent from the lavender in the new garden. The sun shown on the ripening fruit in the valley and everyone waited nervously for the sound of hoof beats.

Finally came a cry from the look-out on top of the house, 'They're coming!'

The entire household assembled in the front garden to greet the King and his court. Tony looked over them all proudly. There could be no finer people in all of England, he thought. Jack rode with the King's party and as the King stepped from his carriage he was escorted by Lady Jane, Jack and the children into the house.

Tony watched the party disappear feeling a little disappointed. It had all been too short. He wondered whether the King had ever seen the portrait he'd commissioned of his faithful giant.

'Oh Tony,' Sebella touched his arm and handed him a feather duster, 'I've told the upstairs servants that you'd dust that high tester on the Golden Bed but then I forgot to tell you! Can you hurry and see to it? It would be a scandal if His Majesty were to have cob webs over his head tonight!'

Tony hurried upstairs and along the wide corridor with its many windows to a large bedroom. The ceiling was covered in plaster flowers and bows and there were plaster sunflowers over the doors. Over the fireplace carved fruit and more flowers surrounded a large painting of the goddess Diana with her bow and arrows surrounded by fat little cherubs. Why did everything have to have those cherubs, he wondered in disgust.

Tony went to the large four poster bed. It had been carved in Spain by monks and covered in gold leaf for Catherine of Aragon on her wedding to King Henry VIII. Henry's daughter, Queen Elizabeth, herself had given it to Sir Richard Grenville for fighting the Spanish navy in his ship, The Revenge. Lady Grace had told him all about the Grenville history. Truly a king's bed.

Sure enough, dust and cobwebs hung from the wide cornice that went around the top. Tony took the feather duster Seb had given him and began to carefully dust the deep carving. He was thinking about Grenville history, whether he liked this new house at all, and cherubs when from behind him came a small cough.

Turning around Tony found himself facing the King who stood with his servant and Jack, who was trying hard not to laugh. Deeply embarrassed, Tony bowed, thrusting the duster behind his back.

'What king has ever had such a subject?' Charles asked merrily. 'Antony Payne, it is indeed good to see you again.'

Tony bowed again with a sweep of the duster like a sword and said, 'Your Majesty, your servant!' They all laughed and Tony glowed with the feeling that Charles hadn't forgotten his friends now that he was king. But as he took his leave he hoped that Jack wouldn't tell Lady Jane of this folly.

The King's secretary made a note of how the King was amused to find Antony Payne dusting the tester of the Golden Bed at Stowe.

CHAPTER 12
BLACKTHORN WINTER

It had turned wet and cold again even though it
was April. A 'blackthorn winter' the women said
as they scurried to take in their wet laundry. The
profusion of white blossom on the blackthorn hedges
meant bad weather ahead. Frosty gales shook the

windows and stripped the blossoms from the apple trees. The Cornish spring held back.

Sebella pulled her winter cloak and hood tight around herself as she walked up the cobbled street from the market. Tony and Seb were now living as caretakers of the little used Stratton Manor, to live out their days in peace and quiet as Jack had told them. Now she opened the small door in the tall, thick wooden gates and fought to close it behind her. Shaking the rain from herself she opened the door to the kitchen.

'Don't remember us having springs like this in the old days,' she grumbled. 'Seems like the seasons are all out of place.' She hung her wet cloak on a peg and pulled up a stool by the fire.

Tony sat contentedly with his pipe and a tankard of hot mulled ale.

'Who had to go to market this morning to have a gossip with the ladies?' he teased. 'And just who had to go out, no matter the weather, to see what new gadget from far off places might be on the traders' carts or what scandals they're printing in the pamphlets?'

'Oh that'll do!' she laughed, taking a sip from his hot drink.

'Jack stopped by while you were out. He said it was just to check and see that I was still keeping the place tidy but you could see he was fair to bust with some news,' he chuckled and drew on his long white clay pipe.

Seb waited but he just looked thoughtfully into the fire.

'Tony Payne! What was his news?' she finally demanded.

'Oh, well,' he came out of his little dream and continued. 'It seems that Master Charlie has gone and done himself proud, fighting those Turks over round Vienna. Distinguished himself in battle, Jack said, and him only a boy of twenty some.' Tony shook his head and smiled again into the fire.

'Oh yes,' he went on, 'remember the painting that fellow started of me all those years ago? Well, he's finally finished it.'

'Now how's he going to do that when he doesn't know what you look like now?' Seb asked, surprised. She couldn't even think how old Tony would have been then, but he was an old man now.

'No,' he laughed at her, 'that artist did the likeness, he just didn't get around to the background and such. Seems the King had him working on so many heads that he only just had time to do the face and hands before getting on with the next. Besides,' he reminded her, 'he was to paint me life size.' He beamed proudly.

'Where is it?' she asked. 'I'd so like to see it, Tony.'

'Forgot to ask. But I'm a-feared it would be a hard journey for us old 'uns, Seb,' he smiled at her lovingly. 'I'll tell you about when he came to paint me, shall I?'

'While I get your dinner,' she patted his knee. It made him young again to tell his stories of the old days. How kind of Jack to come by and tell him his news.

Outside the wind blew the rain against the tiny diamond shaped panes of the windows. A cloud of smoke gusted out of the chimney and hung in the air like a friendly ghost as if to listen to the giant's tale.

Tony died peacefully in his own bed in Stratton in 1691 at the age of 81, four days after Sebella's death. He was so big that they had to cut a hole in the floor of his room to lower his body. His death was registered at St Andrew's Church in Stratton and it was said that he was buried inside beneath the aisle as a mark of respect.

In 1888 as men were removing the flooring in the church to put in new supports, they found a large lead coffin over seven feet long beneath the south aisle of the sanctuary. Inside were the remains of a remarkably large man. Because they found no markings to identify him, however, they reburied the coffin in an unmarked grave and made no note as to where it was.

Tony Payne was a combination of a storybook giant and historical hero, a legend in his own lifetime. He lived for almost a century through some of the greatest changes in England's history and you can still imagine him telling his stories by the fire on a chilly night in Stratton.

BIBLIOGRAPHY

Bayley, Joyce. *A Short History of the Church of St Andrew.* Holsworthy: Bude Printing Co. 1968.

Dew, Rev. R. *A History of the Parish and Church of Kilkhampton.* London: Wells, Gardener, Darton & Co, Ltd. 1926.

Falkus, Christopher. *The Life and Times of Charles II.* George Weidenfeld & Nicholson, Ltd. 1972.

Greener, Rev. W. *Kilkhampton Church.* Bude: J. Gunner (no date)

Latham, Robert, ed. *The Illustrated Pepys,* Bungy: Bell & Hyman Ltd. 1979.

Morgan, Eileen. *Sir Beville Grenville of Stowe.* Ilfracombe, Devon: Arthur H. Stockwell, Ltd. 1969.

Trinick, Michael. "The Great House of Stowe", *Journal of the Royal Institute of Cornwall.* Vol, viii, part 2, pp. 90 - 108. 1979

Watson, D. *The Life and Times of Charles I .* George Weidenfeld & Nicholson, Ltd. 1972.

Young, Jimmy. *A Short History of Ale.* North Pomfret: David & Charles. 1979 St. Ives

With thanks for all their support and contributions to Sir Dudley Stamp, John Hough, Margaret Trewin, Dee Blatchford, Sandy and Tim Dingle and most especially Timothy Pain.

Printed in the United Kingdom
by Lightning Source UK Ltd.
134357UK00001B/73-102/P